and MARRIAGE

How to Guide for Sex, Passion and Desire for Married Couples

Discover the 10 Ways to Turn Your Sex Life from Routine to Lustful Desire

ROCHELLE FOXX

GET YOUR
FREE GIFT!

WAIT! – DO YOU LIKE FREE BOOKS?

My **FREE Gift** to You!! As a way to say **Thank You** for

downloading my book, I'd like to offer you more **FREE**

BOOKS! Each time we release a NEW book, we offer
it first to a small number of people as a test - drive.
Because of your commitment here in downloading my
book, I'd love for you to be a part of this group. You can

join easily here → **http://www.rochellefoxx.com**
If you're interested in having an *outstandingly passionate*

relationship in all areas you **MUST** signup for these

FREE BOOKS! It's easy to join just by going to

my website → **http://www.rochellefoxx.com**

TABLE OF CONTENTS

FOREWORD

I know what you want. Deep down, underneath those mountains of dirty socks and youngster's clothes riddled with impossible grass stains, wadded up grocery lists, PTA meetings, mini-van carpooling trips filled with screaming kids and their sticky fingers on the way to yet another soccer practice. Underneath the boring monotony of every day life, your inner vamp is waiting to be unleashed. You look at your partner, the one you have shared your every early morning coffee with, and you just want them to know you. Not just pass you in the hall and give you a half-glance through a sleepy-eyed gaze, but know you, see you, and feel your innermost needs and desires.

Deep down under the weight that grows heavier with the pressures of each passing day, you're looking for adventure, excitement, and basically counting every single piece of green on your single neighbor's lawn, am I right? Before you decide to throw in the kerosene-soaked towel, light a match and watch it burn, stop fantasizing about that fictitious Fabio to come knocking on your door, because he can't do anything for you. Train your eyes on that man that sleeps next to you night after night, change the oil in that motor of yours, start the engine, and get it purring once again. Revolutionizing your relationship begins in the heart, and the battle is won between the sheets.

At some point or another, every relationship has its ups and downs. Feeling stuck in a rut can affect not only you, but those around you as well. It can put a heavy strain on you and your partner, on a physical as well as emotional level. But don't fear-help is here. In this guide, you will learn simple and easy steps to getting your relationship out of the rut, off the sidelines, and back in the action. In this book, you will discover:

- The Importance of Sex Within Your Relationship

- Tips, Tricks, and Strategies: Turn Your Sex Life from Routine to Peel-Me-Off-the-Ceiling Phenomenal

- Putting Your Plan into Action: Tips for communicating your secret desires within the bedroom, so that your relationship will flourish outside of the bedroom

Great sex begins with throwing off the bowlines of inhibitions, and exploring the deep ocean of sexual possibility. So take a deep breath, grab your partner's hand, and dive in.

Part I:

THE IMPORTANCE OF SEX

Chapter One:

MAINTAINING YOUR FOUNDATION

Strengthening Your Bond

Falling in love is an amazing feeling. The rush you get from meeting your partner for the first time, wanting to know anything and everything there is to know about the one who has captured your heart. Losing sleep because your mind is working overtime to fill itself with thoughts of that one person who makes your heart beat with passion. But what happens when that feeling fades, as inevitably, it will? What happens when you discover all that you can about that person, and you plummet back to reality? Too often, couples make the mistake of thinking that once the initial feeling of being in love fades, it means that they are no longer in love with one another. This is not the case. When you discover cracks in the foundation of your house, do you go out and get a new house? Leave the memories of the life you built there behind? No.

A good relationship needs roots. At its foundation, there should be a special connection interspersed with a solid friendship, because anything less would be too shallow to survive long-term. Imagine for a moment that your relationship is like a tree. The deeper the roots, the stronger the tree will grow. Sex should not be the base of that tree itself, but instead, sex within the relationship should be like watering the roots of that tree. A strong emotional connection is sustenance for a relationship. And sex is the sustenance for that connection; it feeds and strengthens the bond between lovers.

When two people, very much in love with one another, become sexually intimate, the chemistry that you share explodes. The bond that you share with one another grows with time, and the more intimately you get to know the person you are spending your life with, the more amazing the sex becomes. With time, you come to know the ins and outs of your partner: their likes, their dislikes, their little quirks and habits in and out of the bedroom, and just the same, they come to know you. There is a wonderful sense of security to be found in a relationship that has blossomed and deepened over time. However, a deepened relationship also comes with a risk of complacency. The more you grow in love, the more comfortable you become with one another. Comfort can prove a risk to the excitement of sexuality.

Why More Relationships Are Failing

Many troubles can arise in a marriage. Often times, one or both spouses have difficulty leaving work at work, and more often than not, the stress at home increases as a result. Financial troubles have oft been cited as one of the leading causes for divorce. However, despite the many reasons many couples ultimately choose to go their separate ways, if you look hard enough, one problem lies at the heart of each and every issue: the emotional bond between spouses weakens, and ultimately severs. True, you cannot survive on love alone. However, when you maintain an unbreakable bond with your spouse, you can stand strong against any of life's struggles. The number one way to maintain that bond is through emotional and physical connection. Placing a high importance on maintaining your connection begins with rearranging your priorities.

Many marriages fail because the struggles of life get in the way, and couples forget to prioritize. Kids, stress, jobs, the house, bills…they forget to put the needs of their spouse first, and thus, sex gets put on the back burner. First, the amount of times you have sex with your partner in the span of a week lessens more and more, until your sex life becomes sparse, even non-existent.

The further you push sex down on your priority list, the more endangered your relationship becomes. Before you can pull your relationship out of the sexual ditch, you and your partner must get to the root of the problem.

One of the biggest roadblocks that stand between your relationship and having amazing sex is the stressors of life. Life is, in a word, exhausting. At the end of a busy day, sometimes all we want to do is curl up in our nice warm beds, shut the world out, and have a nice long sleep. Sometimes the last thing on our minds is the very thing that will pull us back from the rut: sex. Even when couples do seem to find the time in their day, even some relaxing distractions can get in the way by disguising themselves as leisurely activities. For instance, electronic devices such as the computer, cell phone, iPad, and iPod, etc. These things, while seemingly harmless at first, can take our attention off of our significant others and become detrimental to our relationships by stealing from our personal, intimate time that we share with one another.

Many couples lose sight of the fact that it takes a captain and a co-captain to safely pilot the vessel of a relationship. When two people share a common goal, and keep their eyes on that goal, they stand a much greater chance of succeeding together. When they work against each other, it is like trying to ride a two-person bicycle with each driver trying to move in the opposite direction.

Eventually, it will lead to the demise of the relationship, but not before bridges are burned, walls are built, and feelings are hurt.

Smart couples don't buy into the myth that sex isn't an important aspect of a loving and lasting relationship. They don't put their sex life on the back burner, and they don't let life stop them from emotional and sexual fulfillment. They prioritize. You cannot buy a plant and just leave it in the corner, without ever watering it or exposing it to the sunlight, and expecting it to produce fruit. Just the same, a relationship cannot survive without both parties working to nurture it. Putting your partner's needs above your own will help to build trust, strengthen your existing connection, and nurture your relationship.

Chapter Two:

Understanding Differences How Men and Women View Sex Differently

Men and women are wired very differently. That much is apparent from how we interact with one another. However, having regular sex is important because it unites us in our differences. It has often been said that women require a reason before getting into bed with a man, while men just require the bed. So to speak. To be frank, there is a lot of truth to that theory. Women, by nature, are softer creatures and tend to seek out love, or the possibility of love in a potential partner. Women look for security because they want to feel safe in the knowledge that their heart, as well as their needs, will be taken care of on every level by the man that they choose.

At the same time, men are hunters. They are chemically wired to be natural providers, while women are wired to be nurturers. It's science. Now, of course everyone is different. However, the male gender as a whole view logic, reasoning, and the all-encompassing physical world as primary on their everyday to-do list, while getting in touch with their feelings, and all that the emotional world entails is, much to the female chagrin, secondary. Men tend to view sex as a primal urge, a necessity. Eat, sex, sleep. However, men need sex because, like a stubborn lid stuck tight on a pickle jar, sex frees up a man's ability to truly experience and become aware of his feelings.

Have you, as a woman, ever had a rough day, and you attempted to relay that day's events to your man, only to be met with a distracted spouse listening with half an ear? Before you stick him on the couch for the night, consider that the reason behind his distant demeanor is due to the fact that men are performance-oriented. They become so focused on their goals on a day-to-day basis. This can lead to a man momentarily becoming hardened or desensitized to the love he has for his woman. Sex is a way of refreshing his memory. A man's chemical makeup, in regards to love and sex, is akin to becoming so consumed with every day life that you lose touch with an old friend. Sex, for a man, is like that phone call reaching out to your old friend in order to catch up and reminisce on the bond the special bond that you share.

For women, being the emotional creatures that we are, it is sometimes difficult for us to understand that sex truly is a necessity for our men. Our minds tend to automatically jump to the conclusion that for them, sex is the bottom line. This is simply not the case. Sex is not all that men want from their life partner, and in fact, men want love just as much as we do. Sex is simply fuel for a man's chemical makeup, and the tool that they use in order to find that love from deep within. Experiencing the emotional aspects that the world of sex offers is a perk for a man. Just the same, women tend to view the emotional experience of sex as about 99% of the pie of physical love, while that 1% of physical need is a mere sliver of the experience.

Whereas sex is a doorway to love for men, love is a doorway to sex for women. Think of love as giant safety net that the woman feels comfortable enough to fall into. Once she feels safe and comfortable, she can fall as freely as she wants because she knows that she will find emotional fulfillment. Once she does, she can open herself up to finding sexual fulfillment. No holds barred. This is where the differences can come into play when you find that your relationship is stuck in a rut.

Understanding the differences between men and women is the first ingredient to achieving great sex. If you find that your relationship is hitting a low point, as all relationship sometimes do, it can be difficult for women to truly see the importance of sex. The reason being, that when the relationship vessel hits the rocks, distance created between you and your partner is almost inevitable. Since men view sex as a way of reconnecting with their feelings, they will want to use sex as a lifeline. A way of patching up the holes and getting that ship back out to sea where it belongs. Men will use sex as a way of getting close to their partner. However, this can be difficult for a woman, as she needs to feel close to her partner in order to fully give herself to him.

There is also a significant difference in how sex is physically experienced between men and women. Women tend to experience pleasure through a slow and steady buildup. For a woman, the higher the increase in sexual tension, the more pleasure she derives from sex. Whereas for her, the pleasure increases the more the tension builds, the man tends to experience his pleasure the most during the climax of sex. As a general rule, people are initially self-centered. We know what we want, and we tend to assume our partner wants the same thing we do. A woman likes a slow and steady buildup, and tends to think that her partner automatically knows her desires.

Without first understanding these unique differences, the relationship will become endangered, because the man will give in to his natural urge to seek instant gratification, leaving his woman feeling unsatisfied and wanting. If the problem of miscommunication in the bedroom persists, it is at risk of leaking out into other areas of the relationship, and creating problems in many other areas as well. If you take a moment to appreciate your partner's unique makeup, you can pull your relationship back from the brink of destruction, while achieving the best sex of your life, no matter what stage your relationship is in.

Men's Secret Sexual Fears

It goes without saying that women are often self-conscious about their bodies, no matter what their shape and size, which can hinder their self-confidence in the bedroom. But since men are sexually driven, you may be surprised to learn that they, too, have secret fears about their sexual performance. In the beginning, men worry about your previous sexual partners and how they compare. In size, shape, girth, performance, etc. In addition, men often worry if you are thinking about your previous partners. If we don't moan loudly enough, if we don't show our enthusiasm, men's minds tend to wander. They sometimes worry that we are mentally comparing them to our ex-lovers, and they wonder how they "measure up" in our minds. Are we wishing that we were with Bob instead of Fred? Did George do it better than John? What if she's lying? What if Bill was the best she's ever had? Is she thinking of Eduardo right now? The list goes on.

With time, the more you and your spouse build an intimate connection, the more confident he becomes in his abilities in the bedroom. However, as the years pass and the sex becomes stale, the old fears begin hiding around corners just waiting to pop out at him. Guys often worry about their size, and how they compare to other men. A man's size is a direct link to his ego, and as tough as men are, their ego, as a general rule, is delicate and easily bruised. You should always take special care with a man's ego, especially where sex is concerned. Don't make him feel as if he has to compete with your ex lovers in your mind (the same goes for men, as well). Make sure to shower him with compliments, and show him that you desire him and him alone. This may seem silly at first, but as easily as a man's ego can be damaged, it can be just as easily stroked back to life.

You may be surprised to learn that you are not the only one concerned about your body. In fact, many men can be just as worried as a girl generally is about those few extra pounds he may have gained, and whether or not it shows. Men are just as vulnerable about the way that they look, and they fear that maybe you won't want them as much because of the extra weight they may be carrying around. Just as we women like to be told that we are beautiful, even on our worst days when our hair is all a mess, men like to be reassured that we find their bodies attractive. If you want him to lose a few extra pounds, don't nag him about exercising or going to the gym. This will only serve to again damage his ego, and possibly dig his heels in to resist. Instead, bring up the idea that you yourself would like to lose weight, and that maybe the two of you can join a gym as a healthy way of trying something new together.

Another fear that men tend to worry about in the bedroom is their speed. They worry that their endurance isn't strong enough to keep you satisfied, and again their minds begin to run wild and when you can't achieve an orgasm, or they think you may be faking it, they worry that you are again thinking of a previously lover who could please you. And since men are so sexually driven, in their minds, if they find out that an ex lover could please you and they can't, you may as well just punch them in the nether regions. Men will do and think of anything to try and prolong the sexual experience for you.

However, sometimes his insecurities can get in the way so much so that he loses his erection. When this happens, take a breather for a few moments and stroke his ego as you are stroking him. Believe it or not, most men are worried about whether or not you have an orgasm, and if they can't please you sexually, it makes them feel as if they are less in not only their own minds but yours as well. Remind him of all the things that turn you on about him, and do this with enthusiasm. When he feels secure in the fact that not only is he your number one, but the only one who can please you, it won't be long before he will be back on track.

That being said, one of the greatest fears a guy can have is losing his erection in the middle of the action. For a man, it is like dropping his guy in the middle of the battlefield. When a man loses his erection, a lot of times women take it personally. This only makes the situation worse. Try to remember that a lot of factors can come into play. More often than not when a man loses his erection, it does not mean he has lost his sexual attraction to you. He could be nervous or stressed out over something that happened earlier in the day, or he maybe he had one too many drinks.

Whatever the case may be, it is best to not take an angry or hurt offense to it, and let the situation go completely. Don't try to talk about it with him and figure out what's going on. Chances are, he was already worried about it to begin with, and if you bring it up, he may become upset and withdraw from you. Instead, kiss him on the cheek and tell him it's perfectly fine, roll over, and turn on the television. Cuddle up on his chest to watch your favorite shows, and lightly stroke his skin with your fingertips. This will help him to relax, and before long he'll be back in the game for round two.

What Turns Men On

Although most men will never admit it, their desires run a little deeper than wanting a woman to show up naked in a trench coat. Granted, most men would not turn down such a visitor. Truthfully, it does not take a lot to excite a man. But deep down, a man desires a little something more than simply being touched in his. Men desire to be loved and accepted, just as much as women do. Men don't always exhibit their desires, because they are not naturally in-tune with them like women are. Men derive love and acceptance from the sexual response of their woman.

Men love it when a woman takes an active interest in sex. When they are not always the one to initiate sex, it excites them and makes them feel wanted. When she responds positively to his touch, he views her reaction as validation that he is wanted and needed. Have you ever heard your man ask you why you are not more vocal in the bedroom? The sound of your sexual response to his techniques is exciting to a man because it lets him know that he is accomplishing his goal.

First and foremost, a man is aroused by who you are as a woman. To a man, the touch of a woman's softness is his lifeline to tenderness and vulnerability that he wouldn't otherwise be able to get in touch with. It allows him to open himself up to his own sensitivities, and provides the missing contrast of beauty and femininity to his rough masculinity. A man craves a woman because she complements him, and during sex, he finds in her the parts in him that he lacks.

There are a few simple tricks of the trade to spice up and sustain your man's arousal. Whereas women are sensitive to touch, tone of voice, the feeling of breath upon skin, men are visual creatures. Remember the trench coat? The number one way a man's arousal is enticed is through your appearance. If you want to turn your man's head, and keep your relationship out of the ditch, make taking care of yourself high on your list of priorities. All men are different, but with time, you learn what your partner likes. It may sound age-old, but there is definite truth to the theory that if you continue to keep up your appearance for your partner, he will continue to be appreciative, because it shows that you appreciate him, and care about his desires. An appreciated man is a happy man who tries hard to please his woman.

Kissing is a little-recognized intimate act that goes a long way during foreplay. Like sex itself, kissing is a major act of intimacy. Have you ever noticed that a guy can have sex without feeling, but that kissing seems like a much bigger deal to him? This may seem a bit confusing, and rightfully so, because to women, sex is internal and therefore a definite big deal. However, kissing is more of an intimate act than even sex for a man because the art of kissing alone is highly sensual.. Sex alone is pleasure-oriented.

Unfortunately, for a man at least, sex can be had with or without feeling. But a kiss? A kiss is not merely the opening act for a sexual concert. In one deep, sensual kiss is to convey all feeling that the tongue fails to put into words. The intimacy of a kiss lies in laying your heart bare to another. I

The sad reality is that with the day to day stresses of married life, the intimate act of kissing can become a lost art. Passionate kisses often get replaced by simple pecks on the cheek, or the routine kiss goodnight. If you and your partner have lost touch with the simple act of kissing, now is the time to reconnect those lips, and when you do, make sure you pack the punch of pent-up feelings into one long, steamy kiss.

What Turns Women On

The key to a woman's arousal is much more complicated than a man's. Where as a man is attracted to a woman's softness, a woman is attracted to a man's masculinity because it represents the parts of her that are missing: the strong protector. While a man's ultimate goal during sex is to release his sexual tension, a woman's goal is to feel consumed within the sexual experience, prolonging her excitement for as long as possible, because the more excitement that is built up within her, the more fulfillment she gets out of sex. A woman wants the luxury of lingering within the feeling of her desire for as long as possible.

Women are sensitive creatures, especially to touch and texture. Whereas a man is goal-oriented, and keeps his eye on the orgasmic finish line, a woman seeks to take in the entirety of the experience, and relish in the feel of her lover's hands upon her skin. The longer you are able to tease your woman, the more heightened her arousal becomes. You can stroke her skin and caress her softly as you breathe upon her neck, kiss and nibble at her ears, and just plant soft kisses on her body.

While men are visual creatures, and can easily be turned on at the sight of a naked woman, a woman is a little different. Yes, we can get turned on at the sight of a man's chest, but we generally need a little more fuel to fan the fire. We are highly in tune with our senses, and in addition to being sensitive to touch and texture, we are auditory creatures as well. We are suckers for simple romance, and we like the feel of your breath upon our skin as you whisper pretty words into our ears.

However, don't stop at whispering sweet little nothings. Sometimes women enjoy a little dirty talk. We spend our days catering to our bosses at work, catering to our husbands and our children when we get home. We make sure that the paperwork is done and filed, and that our families are healthy and fed. And though we love our families and our thankful for our jobs, sometimes we just want our big, strong men to sweep us away and love us so well that we forget for one night that we are anything other than your own sexual vixen.

Erogenous Zones

You can arouse your partner sexually by softly caressing any part of your spouse's body. However, it is best to be aware of the different erogenous zones; the sensitive areas on the body that, when touched specifically, heighten your sexual arousal. Just as with possessing differing views on sex and what turns each other on, men and women have different erogenous zones. In this section, take a moment to not only learn about your partner's special spots, but get to know about your own body, as well. If you aren't acquainted with your body and what turns you on, how can you expect your partner to know? When you have a better understanding of what buttons on your own body make you purr, you will gain the necessary confidence to communicate your wants and needs to your partner.

Pleasing a woman is no easy task for a man. There are the basic erogenous zones that the majority of the human population is well aware of, there are also those little hidden hot spots of pleasure that can make woman go from merely agreeing with you in the bedroom to praising you so loud, that you'll be nervous to look your neighbor in the eye the next morning.

Men love boobs. But, a woman's breasts are much more that just fun to play with. They are also home to one of her most sexually sensitive areas: the areolas. The little area around a woman's nipples is delicate, and when teased, can give off intense pleasure. Some women can even achieve orgasm from nipple stimulation alone. As with the vulva, when your breasts become sexually stimulated, they swell, making them more sensitive and thus, more susceptible to achieving orgasm. A breast orgasm is a fascinating concept, and for many, can be achieved. A breast orgasm can be achieved much the same way as a clitoral orgasm, when stimulated by your partner's tongue and fingers.

Aside from Clitoris Headquarters, where the majority of a woman's sexual pleasure emanates from, the G-Spot is the most coveted, yet highly elusive erogenous zone. Although each woman is different, typically the G-spot is located near the roof of the vagina, and is reached when stroked from the inside. Stimulation of the G-Spot can lead to intense pleasure and more powerful orgasms. However, not every woman has ever experienced pleasure from this zone, and many have never even found it. So if you count yourself among these women, there is no need to feel as if your body is flawed. Many women never experience it, and there are many other zones to explore in order to reach intense orgasm.

The perineum is the little area of skin between the thighs that separates the vagina and anus. When stimulated, can also give off intense bouts of pleasure. This zone can be explored in a number of ways. When your partner is performing oral sex on you, they can tease this zone with their fingers. The zone can also be stimulated from certain sexual positions that allow your partner to have access, most particularly from the doggy-style position. While some men think that the anus and the area around it is pleasurable only for women, the perineum is an often overlooked erogenous zone for men, as well.

The navel is another erogenous zone that often doesn't receive the attention that it deserves. The navel has a direct line to your groin, so touching, kissing, or licking the area in and around your navel can heighten your arousal. Licking the navel sends little pangs of pleasure to the genitals for both men and women, and both licking and fingering the navel will remind your partner of oral sex. Make sure that the next time you are performing oral sex on your partner, as your kissing your way down their stomach to their groin, that you make a pit stop to gently tease their navel.

Physical Benefits of Sex

Not only is a romp between the sheets good for your relationship, but also maintaining a steady sex life helps to boost your immune system and is one of the most fun exercise routines you could ever have. Having sex boosts your confidence; your self-esteem, and yes, regular sex can even help to burn off those calories. There are many surprising health benefits that can be derived from sex:

First and foremost, sex is one of the best ways to relieve the stress of a hectic day. If life is bogging you down with endless chores and monotony, the buildup of stress can come out in dangerous ways: yelling at the kids, a dreaded argument with your husband that could have disastrous results. Having regular sex provides an outlet for the stress buildup at the end of each day.

Say goodbye to the age-old headache fake-out, ladies. An orgasm a day will keep those pesky headaches away, and achieving orgasm is a lot more fun than remembering to eat those fruits and veggies. Because having an orgasm releases muscle tension, having sex regularly can actually relieve the cloying pain of a headache, muscle aches throughout your body, and even weaken the strength of a migraine.

Emotional Benefits of Sex

The benefits of sex are numerous, and most can't even be labeled. However, probably the most import list of benefits to sex falls under the emotional category. Sex is uniting. It can put an end to many an argument. Mad at your man? Don't feel like "giving him what he wants"? Don't use sex as a weapon or a means to punish your man. In fact, there are many benefits to having sex while mad at your man. Angry sex is, in a word, awesome. It is much more fulfilling than taking out your aggression on one another in a back and forth argument full of hot air, like an overheated hours-long air hockey competition.

In addition to boosting your emotional connection with your partner regardless of the state your relationship may be in, sex can also boost your self-esteem. Having great sex that is both physically and emotionally fulfilling can enhance your confidence and make you feel good about yourself. When someone wants you just as much as you want him or her, it creates a powerful feeling of assurance in your sexuality. A boost in your confidence sexually will lead to an overall improvement your confidence socially.

Improvement in your sex life can also improve your overall mood. Great sex is a sure fire remedy for sadness and depression, as sex gives you endorphins and acts as a natural antidepressant. Sex not only helps to lessen physical pain, but emotional pain as well. Reconnecting with your partner can help to ease pain and resentment that has built up over trials you and your partner have endured together. Whatever the reason you and your partner find yourselves in a sexual rut, the only way to fix it is to have more sex and work to improve and or restore that deep connection.

Depending on the cause of the rift, sex can help to heal you and your partner emotionally. Once the emotional healing begins, your overall relationship will improve drastically.

Part II:

ORGASM 9-1-1

Chapter Three

ALL ABOUT THAT O, BOUT THAT O, NO FAKERS

A woman being loved right is a happy woman, and she wears a smile that can't be duplicated.

"Fake it til You Make it' Doesn't Apply Here"

Never fake an orgasm. Even if you are afraid of damaging his ego, ultimately, by faking pleasure, you risk damaging the relationship as a whole. Faking an orgasm can be more detrimental to your relationship, as it builds up resentment in you. Eventually, that resentment will show, and it can come out in other ways toward your partner. And if he eventually realizes he isn't the stallion in bed that he thought you saw him as, it can create trust issues. It puts him at risk of becoming withdrawn and less interested in pleasing you. Instead, be honest and upfront with your partner.

Men like to please their women, truly please them. It makes them feel like more of a man. Plain and simple. Be vocal about what you want with your partner. Be assertive, and it will ultimately lead him to respect you more, as well as try harder to ensure your orgasm. If you find that the sex is less than pleasing, you can turn the issue around and use it as a bonding tool for you and your partner. There is no reason that only one partner should achieve sexual fulfillment. By faking an orgasm, you are not only lying to your partner, but also building a permanent residence of sexual frustration for yourself. Sex doesn't have to be fulfilling to only one partner. It takes more time and effort to fake an orgasm. So stop wasting precious time, take your partner's hand, and get down to business. The two of you can journey together to the root of the problem and discover new techniques to help improve your ability to orgasm during sex.

Clit Chat

For a man, reaching orgasm can be like turning on a light switch. Women are not quite so easy to please, especially in the bedroom. Attempting to pleasure a woman can sometimes feel, for both parties, that the man went on a trek up Mount Everest and left his map at home. This section will attempt to explain a few techniques to help a man find his way around a woman's magical little hot button: the clitoris.

The clitoris is the center of a woman's pleasure. The clit is a bundle of over 8,000 nerve endings, at least twice the amount of the nerve endings located in the man's penis, which is made up of about 4,000. This tiny pleasure button is highly sensitive, and can spread pleasure throughout a woman's entire body. The only problem is, the little button can be quite elusive to a man who does not know where he's going. And we all know how men are with asking directions, so this section will do its best to map out a route for you.

The majority of women cannot have an orgasm through penetrative sex alone. This can be troubling and highly frustrating, so if you are one of these women, you shouldn't feel alone. There are plenty of other ways for a woman to have an orgasm, through oral sex or manual stimulation, which is why foreplay is so incredibly important. But if your spouse doesn't take his time, or for whatever reason isn't at the top of his game in the foreplay department, sex can be somewhat less than enjoyable. But anything can be improved; all it takes is a little time and patience to learn your way around a woman's pleasure spots.

A woman's clitoris is actually very similar to a man's penis. Like the penis, the clitoris is not simply a tiny button; the button is only the visible head beneath the hood. The clitoris actually has a shaft that goes up inside the woman's body, and can be stimulated much the same way as a man's penis. Like the penis, the clitoris comes in many sizes. Some are more hidden beneath the hood than others, which can hinder a woman's sexual pleasure. Each woman is different, and therefore each clitoris is different, so men cannot go off of their past sexual experiences alone when pleasing a woman. Some women enjoy a soft touch, while others require a lot of pressure in order to orgasm. You must have patience and learn what your lover likes. But once you do, learning your way around your woman's body will become second nature to you, and the results will be explosive.

The clitoris is located beneath the hood of a woman's vagina, and is about the size of a pea or the head of an eraser. Like a penis, the clitoris swells when a woman becomes sexually aroused, and the more aroused she becomes, the more visible the clitoris becomes. Like a penis, a clitoris has erectile tissue, and once the clit becomes fully erect, a woman is finally on her way to orgasm. Though you may be shy, it is important to be vocal with your lover about they you want him to touch you, and what stroking techniques you enjoy best. As your spouse works to improve his skills, you should try to focus your mind and concentrate on the way his fingers feel against your skin. As your sexual arousal increases, and you get drawn further into the moment, it becomes easier and more apparent what strokes bring you closer to orgasm.

As I said, each woman is different. Some women enjoy the sweet torture of soft, slow, enticing movements across their clit, while others enjoy rapid rubbing in a back and forth motion, while applying the right amount of pressure. Generally, women take a while to "heat up," and therefore, unless your spouse specifically asks you to dive right in, I suggest beginning your session of love making with slow caresses to entice her passion. The longer you stroke and build her passion, the more intense her orgasm will be.

As a suggestion, depending on the makeup of your spouse's anatomy, you can use one hand to pull back the hood of her clit, or she can hold it for you. Place at least two fingers on either side of her clit and, while applying pressure, rub her clit in a circular motion. You can also try rubbing your fingers slowly and directly over the top of her clit. While you are massaging her clit, try inserting two fingers into her vagina, and applying light pressure downward as you move your fingers in and out. This will give her the same sensations she experiences during sexual intercourse while her clit is being stimulated, which will make her orgasm nearly twice as powerful. With your fingers inside of her, you can also try inserting them all the way, like you would a penis to the hilt, and moving them in a circular motion as you simultaneously stimulate her clit in a circular motion.

You can also try moving your fingers in the motion of a figure eight, making your movements larger to stimulate both the clit and the vaginal lips. You can also try placing a finger on either side of the clit, rubbing your fingers lightly in an up and down motion, again stimulating the vaginal lips in addition to the clitoris. Another technique to try is to spread the vaginal lips apart, and gently tapping the clitoris in a rhythmic motion. This technique may depend on what your woman likes, as each clitoris has a different level of sensitivity, and the direct motion could prove too much for a highly sensitive clit, or one that is already over stimulated.

Remember that the part of the clit that you see, the tiny little nub, is only a fraction of the clitoris. There is still a shaft of pleasure that goes up inside the woman's body, and it can also be used to manually stimulate pleasure. You can place your thumb and forefinger around the shaft of the clitoris; apply gentle pressure, squeezing softly as you stroke the shaft in an upward motion, much like you would manually stimulate a penis. Much like a penis, you can increase the pleasure as you gently increase your speed. You can also try tugging the shaft downward. While you are stimulation the shaft, try softly inserting the tip of your finger between your spouse's vaginal lips. Begin lightly at first, hovering at the vaginal entrance to tease her as the pleasure builds. You can try moving your fingers up and down, or in a back and forth motion. As she gets closer to reaching orgasm, in a swift motion, insert your fingers all the way. The sudden jolt of your intrusion as she reaches her climax will increase the intensity of her orgasm.

Caring for the Penis 101

We previously discussed ways to please a woman during foreplay, but now it's time for your husband to get a little attention. Though it is called a "blowjob," try to clear your mind of relating the act of performing oral sex on a man as a "job." If you think of it as hard work, that is exactly what it will become. As with a woman, each man is different, although there are far less tricks when it comes to giving your man an amazing blowjob. Some men enjoy having just the tip of their penis stimulated with your tongue as you stroke the shaft, and others enjoy oral sex most when you take their whole penis in your mouth.

There are measures you can take to make the experience of a blowjob more pleasurable for the both of you. There are a variety of flavored lubricants to explore and play around with. Since some men do enjoy having their entire shaft stimulated during a blowjob, using a flavored lubricant can help you if you have troubles with your gag reflex. Not to mention, the different flavors of lubricant will help to add spice to your sex life by adding a variety of options for you to try.

There are many ways to use a blowjob to spice up your sex life. Take control. In the morning, try surprising your man by waking him up with an impromptu blowjob, or hand job. A lot of men enjoy sex first thing in the morning. You're sleepy, you're still vulnerable, and let's face it, sex is the best thing to wake up to next to coffee. The best way to get your man ready for morning sex is to perform oral sex on him until he is fully awake and ready to go. When you begin giving your husband a blowjob, you are in charge of his pleasure. If you perform oral sex on your man first thing in the morning, you can enjoy watching his facial expressions as he slowly realizes what's happening while you pleasure him awake.

Remember that as with pleasing a woman, you want to start off slow when giving your man a blowjob. When your man awakens, make sure you maintain eye contact. Eye contact can be a powerful tool in the bedroom. While maintaining eye contact, you can convey more feelings and intentions than your tongue can express. Maintaining eye contact as your stroking your husband lets him know that you want him, and makes his imagination to run wild.

After lubricating his shaft, start stroking your hand up and down as you graze your lips against the tip of his penis, letting the underside of his head slide against your tongue. Make sure to take things slow not only for his benefit, but yours as well. Going to fast can cause your gag reflexes to kick into gear, which can pull you both out of the moment. One tip to try is to place a firm grip (but not too tight) at the base of his penis while you wrap your mouth around the head, connecting your lips with your fist as you gently stroke upward in a rhythmic most. This gives his penis the same sensations as being deep throated, while allowing you to ease into the experience.

A tip for when your jaw gets tired is to brush the tip of his penis against your lips, and then stroke the head against your tongue while continuing to stroke him. This keeps him lubricated as well as sustains his erection. Make sure to not only keep eye contact, but to also let out a few moans, and try humming against his penis periodically throughout. Not only does this let him know that you want him, but the vibrations generated by the feeling of your humming against him will give his penis an extra stimulation.

Another tip to help add to the stimulation is to stick a breath mint in your mouth as you are going down on him. The minty freshness will add an extra little sexy tingle, heightening the sensations for him. Not to mention, it helps to keep the whole experience pleasurable for you. The same can work with either cold water or an ice cube. Anything that gives off a cool, tingly feeling will help to enhance a man's sexual experience during a blowjob. One last important thing to keep in mind: don't neglect your man's testicles. As you are coming to a finish, make sure to lightly caress his testicles. The feel of your touch against his most sensitive area is sure to send your man over the edge.

---

Chapter Four

10 WAYS TO TURN YOUR SEX LIFE FROM ROUTINE TO PEEL-ME-OFF-THE-CEILING PHENOMENAL

Whether you are looking to spice up your marriage and have a little fun, or you feel that you and your partner are in a deep rut and you are concerned for your love's survival, there are many simple and effective techniques to revive your relationship.

The KISS Method

Looking to spice up your sex life? Keep it Simple and Sassy. Creativity is a wonderful thing, but just remember: elaborate creativity does not always equal the goal. Don't spend too much time agonizing over perfection that you forget to enjoy yourself. Keep your eye on the goal, and don't be afraid to tell your partner what you want. A little assertiveness never hurt anyone. In fact, switching up the role with your partner now and then and asserting yourself can be a huge turn-on to your man. Men are direct. If you want to get his attention, you have to speak his language.

You want out of the sexual rut? You want to be taken out on a date? You want to be romanced? Tell him. And once you tell him, follow up your words by showing him. You know that little mantra, "treat others how you would like to be treated"? Try applying that motto to your relationship. If you want him to show you love, show it to him first. You want to revive the passion? When you first wake up, or before he leaves for work in the morning, grab him and give him one of those deep, intimate kisses we were discussing earlier. If you are feeling repressed, grab your man and let out all that pent-up passion in one kiss.

He may be surprised at first and you may hear the words, "Where did that come from?" But if he has a somewhat taken aback reaction, don't let it dissuade you. Be persistent. He may be confused at first, but men want to be wanted. They may not say it or show it as much as women do, but they like it when their woman takes an initiative and actively wants them. Before he walks out that door in the morning, ditch the quick, emotionless peck. Grab the back of his head and press your lips to his. Run your fingers through his hair, and gently massage his scalp. Give him a send-off that will stick in his mind throughout his day.

No matter what kind of day at work he has, it will be at the forefront of his mind when he walks through the front door that evening. He will be chomping at the bits with anticipation to see just where that kiss came from, and if there is more waiting for him when he gets home. If you give him a passionate kiss in the morning, he will have eight hours to let his mind run wild with thoughts of what he wants to do to you when he gets home. To get yourself in the mood, make sure to take a little time throughout the day to fantasize about what he will do to you, and how you plan to please him that night.

Here Today, Gone to Maui

One aspect of a great sex life that is often overlooked by many couples is the importance of spontaneity. I cannot stress this enough: women love a man who is spontaneous. Most men either do not seem to understand this simple fact, or, are too afraid to suck it up and go for it. Spontaneity creates excitement in the midst of an otherwise average weekday.

There are many ways to incorporate spontaneity into your relationship. For starters, you could surprise your lover with an unplanned trip. If there is some place the two of you have always wanted to visit, now is the time to go. Take the initiative and plan a second honeymoon for you and your spouse. Nothing reignites the fire quite like grabbing your lover's hand, leaving the real world behind, and escaping away to paradise for a little while.

A surprise trip is always fun, but unfortunately, you have to return to the reality of everyday at some point. So how do you sustain the passion once you get back? Or if you don't have the money or the means to get the time off just yet, you say? Never fear. There are also many cost-effective ways to get creative with spontaneity. Instead of passing your lover in the hallway, come up behind her, pull her hair aside, and whisper softly against her neck.

Never underestimate the power of the neck kiss. Even the most angry, rigid woman is no match against the sensitivity of her neck. Now, if you are a man reading these words, I have an idea of what you are thinking. "Yeah, right. There is no way I'm setting myself up for that kind of rejection. I'm married to the ice queen. If my lips touch her neck, they'll get stuck." Even so. Man up and go for it. Even the coldest woman will be putty in your hands. The moment that your soft lips touch that sensitive erogenous zone at the base of her neck, your ice woman will transform to a giggling schoolgirl before your very eyes.

Sometimes, merely switching up the location adds a little excitement to a sex life that is growing stale. Maybe you are out with your spouse at a boring social function, such as a mandatory work party. Or maybe it is Friday night, and you and your spouse decided to go catch that new movie you have both wanted to see. Whatever the occasion, the two of you can find a little time for some spontaneous sex. Maybe you're on the car ride home, or you're on your way to that party. Put your hand on your spouse's leg, caress them softly, find a secluded spot, and pull over.

Adding a little spontaneity will get your hearts beating faster. And if you have a little spontaneous sex in a somewhat public place, somewhere where there's at least a hint of a chance of getting caught, it heightens the sexual excitement. Remember when you were teenagers, and you snuck away to be with your first love, hoping against hope that your parents wouldn't discover your tryst and ground you? The possibility of getting caught not only adds a little danger and excitement to the relationship, something that women tend to go weak in the knees for, but it can also make you feel young again.

If you are too shy or nervous to go big, then try staying at home first. Try having sex in a new location, such as the kitchen counter or on top of the washing machine. Women love to be manhandled, and these every day locations are ideal for such a moment. If she's doing the dishes, or folding the laundry, come up behind her and wrap your arms around her waist. Kiss her neck. Turn her around, grab her behind, lift her up...and I am positive you can take it from there. If you have kids and worry they will catch you, then wait until the kids are asleep. As you and your partner are turning out the lights and preparing for bed, pull her into the kitchen or laundry room and remind her that she is yours. Don't worry about the kids. Again, the possibility of getting caught only adds to the excitement.

As a woman, you can add spontaneous excitement to your relationship by creating a sexual tryst as well. If you are in the car and your man is unable to pull over, reach over and manually stimulate him. Surprise him with a spontaneous happy ending. This bold move lets him know that you want him, even if he can't, for the moment, reciprocate the sexual favor. The spontaneity of the moment will thrill your partner, and make them feel as if they are so wanted by you, that you just cannot stand another minute without having them. The thrill of danger and the excitement of the new place combined will spice up an otherwise dulled sex life.

Be My Baby Tonight

One of the best bits of advice I have ever received is a simple statement I will pass along to you: make sure to always date your spouse, especially after marriage. When life gets in the way, we can become comfortable. Just as waking up in the same bed every morning, watching the same television, going to the same job day and day out, pulling into the same driveway each night can lull us into a sense of familiarity, the same can be said for our marriages. When we see the same things day in and day out, the same people, we become complacent in our lives, and before we even realize it, we tend to take them for granted. We get so used to these things being a part of our every day lives that we automatically assume they will just always be there. Thus, our appreciation for them falls to the wayside.

If you don't believe me, try going a day without toilet paper. Suddenly, when you have it again, it becomes invaluable to you. Am I right? Just the same, unfortunately, we don't always appreciate the invaluable role people have in our lives until they are suddenly gone. This is an especially sad case when that person is our spouse. Let us break the cycle now. One way to do that, is to actively take an interest in our significant others. Do you ever feel downtrodden because you feel as if your partner just doesn't see you? Do you feel that he passes you over these days, like he is just going through the motions when he looks at you? Rather than arguing, fighting, and complaining that he just doesn't see you anymore, stop. Show him who you are. Show him that you are still that woman who is still in love with her man.

It may seem like common sense, but relationships are a give and take. If you feel your husband is not noticing you, give him something to notice. As I stated before, men are not always in tune with their feelings. As tempted as we are to send them little hints and hope that they can read our minds, I am going to tell you right now. They can't. Stop becoming angry and frustrated with them because you didn't put a crystal ball on their grocery list, so they didn't go out and get one. Men don't understand hints. They understand what is in front of them. Be up front and direct with your spouse. Tell them what you want. If nothing changes, then nothing changes, and since women are relationship-oriented, we are more in tune with our emotions and our feelings, and what needs fixing in that area. The change begins with you.

Remember your first date? The second? Remember that honeymoon phase when your relationship was brand new, the butterflies you felt in your tummy as you hummed to yourself while you put extra care into your makeup for that special date night with that amazing man that you just knew in your heart was 'The One'? In order to revive your relationship, you must first change your attitude. Revive yourself. Take a moment, go into the bathroom, shut the door, and look in the mirror. Pull out your stockpile of makeup, and have a little fun. Play with the colors, and giggle to yourself at the thought of the double take he will have when he sees you.

Dressing up for him will not only kindle that flame that burned bright in the beginning, but you will also be surprised to see what it does for you. Putting extra care into your appearance for your man will also boost your confidence in yourself. It will help you to feel in control and maybe even a little feisty. It will remind him of that girl he first fell in love with. Yes, life gets in the way, and the newness of love fades. But it doesn't have to fade into the boring and mundane. With just a bit of rearranging on your personal priority list, making sure to take care of yourself will give your relationship a boost.

Men. While your woman is going the extra mile to take care of herself just for you, remember that you have this beautiful woman who loves you with all of her heart. If she holds this book in her hands, that means she is doing all that she can to reconnect with you and fix the problem. As I said before, it's a give and take, so do your part. You have her, you won her, so don't ever stop appreciating the fact that you are the champion and she is your woman. Treasure her, and treat her as your prize. Never stop dating her, and always make her feel like she is yours. Your girl. Set aside time each week for a date night. Whether you take her out and show her a special night, or you stay in and cuddle up to a movie by candlelight, either way, if you make her the center of your attention, I guarantee you the location won't matter.

A woman in love won't put all her stock in what a man can do for her, where he can take her, and what he can buy her. What a woman in love wants is simple: she wants the time and attention of the man she loves. She wants to know that she is still what he wants. Designate at least one night a week for a date night for just you and your partner. No phones. No checking e-mail or taking phone calls at the dinner table. Set your attention on your partner, and your partner alone. Take an active interest in getting to know them again. In addition, set aside time each day to let your partner know that they are wanted, because being wanted is just as important to a man as it is to a woman. Let them know what it is you love about them; take time to truly appreciate the qualities that your spouse possesses that first captured your heart.

Don't neglect your partner, and they won't have cause to turn their thoughts and their hearts elsewhere. Once you re-establish the connection that you and your partner share in your every day life, that connection will overflow into the bedroom. There is nothing exciting about methodical sex. Once you put your heart back into the relationship, it will reignite the passion in your sex life.

Time to Play

Approaching your lover with the idea of bringing toys into the bedroom can be complicated. We said before that a man is wired to pride himself based on his performance in every area of life, so at first the idea of toys can have the same effect on a man as having to stop and ask for directions. The orgasm is the mutual destination, and the man is driving. His goal is to get you both to that glorious finish line without help. If you are not careful, it can send the message: My woman doesn't trust me to please her.

However, after you get him to calm down and listen, he will see that the use of sexual toys doesn't have to be deflating to his ego. Your man could never be replaced with a mere toy, and he should be reassured of that. Toys are not capable of loving or physically fulfilling interaction. Toys are merely a means to enhance your sexual experience, and what many men do not understand is that using sexual toys can bring excitement into the bedroom for the both of you. A toy can enhance a woman's pleasure, intensifying her orgasm and even helping it to last longer. Who doesn't like orgasms? The more intense her orgasm is, the more she is going to want another and another. More intense orgasms for her, equal more sex overall for the man.

It can be difficult for a woman to orgasm. In fact, if you have difficulty reaching orgasm, don't feel you are alone. It is more common for a woman to have sex without achieving orgasm than it is for a woman to reach climax through sexual intercourse. If you are a woman who finds sex less enjoyable because of your difficulty reaching orgasm, then the use of sex toys is your new relationship lifesaver. If you want to bring even a little more kink into the use of sex toys, you can let your partner watch you use a vibrator. You would be surprised just how much shared pleasure comes from allowing your man to watch you pleasure yourself.

Exploring your own body and figuring out what you like is natural, but when you add a second pair of eyes to the interlude, it adds a hint of naughtiness, and therefore, heightens the sexual excitement for the both of you. When you are front and center stage, you become the star of your own show for a very special audience: your lover. When he watches you, he becomes enraptured with everything about the moment. When two people are having sex, they can become caught up in the moment and often oblivious to what is going on around them. When you please yourself for your lover, it allows him to take notice of you in a way that he may not have been able to before.

When your man is a mere spectator to your one-woman show, he will see your facial expressions, hear your moans, and watch your movements from the point of view of an outsider looking in. If you really want to get creative, lay down a few rules beforehand: let him know that for this moment, you are the star, and he is not allowed to touch you. Only allow him to explore you with his eyes. This creates a whole new level of erotic admiration for you within him and allows him to fully absorb the sensuality of the moment. Something that men, who are not detail-oriented, are often unable to do. At the same time, watching you please yourself will heighten the anticipation for him, as he is barred from participating. As the anticipation builds, so does his need for you. This teaches him patience, and renews his desire to possess you.

If you are a shy woman, you can still use sex toys to enhance your pleasure without putting the spotlight on you. A vibrator can be used during sexual intercourse to enhance your pleasure while your partner explores your G-spot. There are many ways to use a sex toy, and many toys to introduce into the bedroom. Choosing the right toy for you and your partner can in and of itself be seen as a bonding experience. The excitement of bringing a new experience into the bedroom will help to increase the anticipation. Having a renewed anticipation for sex with your lover helps to also freshen a sex life that has grown stale.

Know Your Position

A great way to rekindle the romance and reignite the passion is for you and your partner to try out new sexual positions. Incorporating new moves into your sex life will help to keep things new and fresh in the bedroom.

Let's begin with a classic crowd pleaser: the "doggy style" position. Doggy style is a classic for a reason: it is the optimum position for hitting your g-spot, it allows the man to reach around and stimulate your clit, and it is one of the best positions for deep penetration. This position is highly arousing, and tends to bring out our most basic, primal urges. The doggy style position is great for rough, passionate sex, but the downside to it is that it doesn't allow for a lot of intimacy, since you and your partner can't maintain eye contact. But it does allow for the man to use his free hands to explore your body as he thrusts, which can maximize your chances to achieve orgasm during intercourse.

A great way to spice up your sex life is to make time to meet up with your spouse for a quickie. Maybe you only have a short break for lunch, and you don't have a lot of time to get down and dirty. Heat up your connection by arranging an impromptu tryst with your partner. If you can find an available coat closet, or a small space to hook up, the perfect position for getting it on in an enclosed space is for partner to stand upright as you rest on a stool, or balance your weight on top of him while leaning against the wall. You can brace your legs against the opposite wall while your husband stands between them, thrusting. This position can be a bit difficult, as with any standing position, but the spontaneity of the moment will be a huge turn-on for you and your partner.

You can add a twist to the position by turning and facing the wall, bending at an angle while your partner grabs your hips, holding you up. This is also a variation on the doggy style position, and if you angle yourself just right, you can achieve maximum penetration. You can also try propping yourself up against a surface, such as a stool, a table, the kitchen counter, a desk, etc., while wrapping your legs around your partner's waist, and grasping him around the neck. The downside to this position is that it requires the man to do most of the work. Since it is a standing position, it is not ideal for maintaining endurance.

Another great option for if you want to get down and dirty with a little spontaneous sex, is to have sex on the stairs. If you have a two-story house, put those stairs to some good use by making time for a little quickie. Sit on the stairs and rest your back up against them, draping your legs against your man's shoulders as he thrusts between them. The angle provided by the stairs will allow you to have deeper penetration. The downside to this position is that whether the stairs in your house are hardwood or carpeted, they can still be quite a bit uncomfortable, and you may not be able to endure this position for long. However, the spontaneity of the moment will be a huge turn on for you and your partner, and if the discomfort proves to be too much, he can put a romantic twist to the moment by lifting you up and carrying you to the bedroom.

One position that is exciting for both the man and woman is the "cowgirl" position, with the woman on top. Men love this position, because it gives them a great view of your body. This position allows the woman to have almost total control, and she can set the pace as fast or slow, as she would like. As we said before, men naturally like to get things done as quickly as possible, and this tends to show in their sex life as well. No muss, no fuss.

When the man switches up the pace, it can make it difficult for the woman to have an orgasm, as some clits are so sensitive that the slightest wrong movement can make a woman lose her orgasm. But when the woman is riding on top, she has complete control of both his and her movements. Not to mention, this position allows the roles to be switched, which can be a major turn on for a man. Some men like it when their woman becomes assertive, and not only show her interest, but actually initiates sex. This position allows the woman to become dominant and show her man that she is in charge. A helpful tip for when trying this position is to spread your legs as far apart as you can get them. This allows for deeper penetration.

A similar sexual position is called the "reverse cowgirl." This position again gives the woman a little more control over the pace, while still allowing the man to exhibit some of the same dominance over his woman as the doggy style position. Reverse Cowgirl also allows the woman to adjust the angle, and is a great option for hitting the woman's g-spot, that elusive little erogenous zone inside of her vagina. This position allows the man to appreciate the curves of his woman from behind, a little more easily than the doggy style position. This position works similarly to being on top; you climb on top of your husband, but facing away from him, as he either lies back on the bed, or sits up on a chair or the couch. This position is a winner with the men, though it doesn't allow for a lot of physical contact and like doggy style, it can be hard on your knees.

Another position that is ideal for hitting the woman's g-spot is called the "magic bullet." This position involves the woman lying flat on her back with her legs raised straight up in the air. The man kneels down and enters her, grasping her legs for leverage while he thrusts into her. This position also allows him to push your legs together, which causes friction between your legs and stimulates your clit as he thrusts in and out. The down side to this position is that it doesn't give the woman a lot of control over the pace, and doesn't allow her to be as active, leaving the majority of the work to the man.

The "squat" is another position where the woman sits on top, again giving her the majority of the control. The woman sits on top of her man with her knees slightly bent, squatting on top of him. She can grab his hands or support herself by leaning on against the mattress, but in this position she raises herself up and down, bouncing on top of him. The difficulty of this position is that it requires you to maintain your balance, which isn't always comfortable for you or visually pleasing to your partner, but when executed correctly, this position gives you some amazing sensations.

One variation of the squat is to kneel in a sitting position on the bed while your partner kneels behind you. Rest your hands on the mattress and as he enters you from behind, you can bounce up and down on top of him. This position is similar to doggy style as well, and also allows for deep penetration. However, since you cannot kiss or look one another in the eyes, it is not as intimate as some of the other positions, but it is perfect for stimulating the woman's g-spot. Like the doggy style position, this one is also fast and very thrilling, so if you are trying to prolong sex and have a list of other positions you would like to try, you may want to save this position until you're ready for the big finish.

The "face-to-face" position is a great position to start off with when you are taking things slow. The slow movements of this position help to build sexual tension, allowing you to feel your partner inside of you. With this position, both partners share equal control over the movements and the pace. This position works by sitting opposite of one another on the bed, while you slide into his lap and he slides into you. You wrap your legs around his waist as he cradles you, rocking back and forth.

The "spider" is a similar position in which you begin facing opposite one another, but lie backward. Each partner then raises their knees up, and you each hold onto the other's legs. You begin moving in slow, slight movements. This position is great for prolonging arousal, and helping to build up a man's stamina. If you are looking for a languid and laid back sex, this is the perfect position to try. The downside to this position is that it doesn't involve a lot of action, and while it can prolong a man's orgasm, it can serve to diminish the passion between you.

The "speed bump" position is similar to doggy style, and is a great position for rough, passionate sex. The woman lies face down on the bed, supporting her pelvis with a cushion or a pillow. The angle created by the pillow will allow for maximum penetration, enhancing her pleasure. If you want sex to last longer, you may want to save this position until the very end. It is a fun, fast position that allows the man to be in the dominant position, and the heat tends to escalate quickly, making this position ideal for those times when you just want hot, rough, and fast sex.

The "galloping horse" is yet another position that allows the woman to have full control. With this position, your husband sits on a chair as you climb on top of him, extending your legs outward on either side of him. You can hold onto the back of the chair, or your husband's shoulders for support as you lean backward, rocking back and forth on top of him. This position allows for deep penetration, enhancing your ability to have an orgasm. Like both the cowgirl and reverse cowgirl positions, it allows your husband to have a front row view of your body, while you have complete control over setting the pace.

One crowd pleaser is a move called the "melody maker." This one is a great option for when you're hanging out with your spouse in the living room. If you have an ottoman or a footstool handy, grab it and get ready to get on your way to a powerful orgasm. For this position, lie on your back across the ottoman, with your head dangling slightly over the side as your husband kneels between your legs. As your husband thrusts, the surge of blood to your head will make for a mind blowing orgasm. The downside to this position is that the rushing of blood to your head can also make you pretty dizzy, so you may not be able to stay in this position for too long.

Let's get back to the classics. The "missionary" position is ideal for making love, and rekindling that intimate connection. One reason that the missionary position is good for maintaining intimacy is because it is the perfect position for you and your spouse to stare into each other's eyes. As your husband is on top of you, you can keep eye contact as he runs his fingers through your hair and strokes your face. The downside to the missionary position is that it doesn't allow for deep penetration. The missionary position often gets a bad rap for being boring and too traditional with minimal action. However, one tip for spicing it up is to wrap your legs around his, instead of around his waist, and arching your back. With your legs around his, you have a bit more control over his speed, and arching your back allows for deeper penetration. Another variation of the missionary position is for you to lie on your back while twisting your hips to the side.

Bend your knees slightly as your husband thrusts between them. This twist is another great position for hitting your g-spot.

Each of you can also lie down on your side, in a sideways version of the missionary position. This position is sensual and erotic, and an easy way to put a spicy spin on a warn-out position. Another variation is to drape your legs over your husband's shoulder while he kneels between them, thrusting into you. This position allows for deep penetration and allows him to run his hands over your body and touch you as he pleases. If you and your husband really want to get racy, he can lean back on his knees, while you wrap your legs around his waist as he lifts you up. This allows him to penetrate you deeper, while grinding against your clit. The more you arch your back, the more access he will have to reach your g-spot. The downside to this position is that it places the work on your husband. It requires him to have the endurance to hold you up while concentrating on thrusting.

One last, amazing twist that you can put on the missionary position is called the "cat." With this position, the woman lies back on the bed while the man climbs on top of her. As he enters you, he can move as far up your body as possible, penetrating you deeply. Then, instead of thrusting, he presses up against you, grinding himself into you as he moves in slow, small circles. This is a great position for women who have difficulty achieving orgasm during sex. With this position, the woman's clitoris is being directly stimulated, while the man's penis caresses her walls, giving her wave after wave of amazing, orgasmic sensations. This requires the man to maintain a slower, steadier pace than he is used to. This technique can also be used in the doggy style position. Although the clit will not be directly stimulated, the man can press up against the woman, grinding himself into her in slow, steady circles as he reaches around to stimulate her clit with his fingers. This massages her walls and gives her the same orgasmic sensations while hitting her g-spot as an added bonus.

"Spooning" is another position that allows for slow, intimate sex. Each partner lies down on the bed, with the man lying behind the woman. He enters her from behind, and together they rock back and forth while in a cuddling position. This position is another that doesn't require a lot of action, but that doesn't mean that the passion is any less present, as this position is great for enhancing the feeling of intimacy between you and your partner.

Having sex while standing up allows you to get creative in a lot of ways, such as having sex anywhere that will give you standing room. For instance, both the kitchen and the shower are great locations for having sex in the standing position, although the trouble with this position is that it does not allow for maximum penetration. Overall penetration in this position can be difficult, and when that happens, it can prove to be a major mood killer. The benefit to this position is that it allows your man to have access to anywhere on your body that he wants to touch, and he can easily reach around your waist to stimulate your clit.

Know Your Role

If you find that sex in your marriage is becoming monotonous, or dulled with routine, try switching the roles up a bit. You can start with role-playing, which allows you and your partner to open yourself up to the fantasies that you have always wanted to try but maybe were too shy to attempt before. Dressing up and pretending to be someone or something else frees up your inhibitions, and allows you to explore your inner desires while taking the heat of embarrassment off of yourself for a bit.

Not to mention, dressing up is fun. Why did we do it on Halloween as children? Because roleplaying adds excitement, right in the middle of the boring and mundane. The only difference as adults is that, the costumes have changed a bit, and the candy waiting for us is much sweeter. And, well, the goal here is to keep our spouses from going door-to-door looking elsewhere for that candy.

There are many different roleplaying scenarios that you can explore with your partner. That is the beauty of roleplaying. Whatever the two of you may be in to, there is going to be something out there to be found just for you. Approach the subject with your partner, and then have fun learning what kind of fun things they would be into. It's a journey the two of you can take together, and the planning process itself can be used as a bonding experience.

One of the most popular roleplaying categories is putting one person in the role of the dominant, and the other in the role of the submissive. Most people, who hear the words dominant and submissive, think of whips and chains and all sorts of items that constitute as freaky and exciting. However, there are many different levels to the dominant and submissive roles, and many different roleplaying scenarios that fall under this category.

You can take the scenario to the extreme (just make sure that your partner is okay with it, and to first set down some ground rules), or you can tone it down while still playing your roles. Many scenarios make up the category of dominant and submissive, and they don't always have to fall under BDSM, or have to involve bondage. Any scenario that involves one person in charge will do. See the list below for a few ideas to jump-start your creativity:

- Boss and Employee: You're late again? Don't want to be written up? Step into my office.

- Prison Guard and Prisoner: Badge. Uniform. Enough said.

- Landlord and tenant: Rent due? Can't pay? You will.

- Doctor and Patient: This scenario can be exciting, because it allows your partner to examine and explore your body as they see fit, and the doctor will see you now.

- Nurse and Patient: Similar to the Doctor/Patient game, but the woman dons a sexy uniform for her man, taking on the dominant role for the evening.

- Pilot and Flight Attendant: Time to put a few miles on your membership card.

- Fireman to the rescue: Firemen are hot. Enough said.

- Master and sex slave: I think you get the idea.

Another possible scenario to spice things up with your partner is to take your games out into the public. Remember when you first met? Do you ever wish you could recreate that moment? Well, why not. One fun scenario for couples to try is to meet up at a restaurant or a bar separately, and role-play as if they have never met before. You could use fake names or pretend that you are meeting your partner again for the first time. Either way, you could walk up to one another and reintroduce yourselves. If you choose to add fake names into the mix, the two of you could sneak off to the bathroom or a coat closet for a quickie. This gives you and your partner the feeling of having a faux one-night stand. This type of tryst helps to act out a secret fantasy, without suffering through the guilty aftermath of a real one-night stand.

If you or your partner enjoys reading, you can get your hands on a piece of erotic literature, and read aloud to one another to slowly turn each other on and heighten the anticipation through each other's imagination. If you or your spouse is shy, reading aloud to one another can also help to jumpstart the flow of talking dirty to your spouse. You could even discover a favorite book together, and use it as a roleplaying guide. You can dress up as your favorite characters in the book, and act out your favorite sexy scenes. If you really want to get creative, you can even use props. If you and your partner are not a fan of reading, or don't want to take the time, you can also incorporate a sexy movie into your tryst and act out your favorite scenes.

Whatever sorts of scenarios you and your partner come up with, remember that the ultimate goal is to add excitement to your relationship. As with approaching the subject of the use of sex toys, the subject of roleplaying, if you aren't careful, can imply to your partner that you are unhappy with the way things are, or that you don't want them the way that they are. To avoid hurting your partner's feelings, be mindful of insecurities that may arise and just remember that discovering new ways to spice up your sex life is a journey for the two of you, a bonding experience designed to help renew the intimate bond that you share.

Sext Me Up

There are all sorts of ways to spice up your sex life with your partner when the two of you have alone time together. But what about those times in the middle of the day, when real life has no choice but to get in the way? Going back to the subject of spontaneity, thanks to modern day technology, there are sexy little surprises you can send to your partner throughout the day. Now, I will state again because I think it bears repeating in this day and age: when you are with your partner, make sure to keep up the communication by putting the phones down. But when you are forced to be away from your partner, you can use the phone to help reignite the passion.

Whether you are a stay at home mom, or a working woman, set aside a little time in your busy day to send your spouse a little surprise texts. If you're at work, you can sneak a bathroom break to take a naughty photo. Just remember to send a text of warning first to let him know that what he is about to see is not safe for work. If you're too shy or unable to take a photo, try sending him naughty little messages about what you want to do to him, or what you want him to do to you. Build up the sexual tension, and then tell him what you plan on doing to him when he gets home. In this way, you will entice him with anticipation, and his mind will be focused on you. He won't be able to focus on much else because his thoughts will already be racing home to you.

Words are a powerful thing. Just the same with a naughty text, it is also important to make sure you take an interest in your partner's day. Check in every now and then with a nice, sweet message just to let him know he is on your mind. Ask him how his day is; tell him you love him, and that you can't wait to see him tonight. Kind and loving words will open airtight seals, and even if you and your partner haven't been communicating well lately, you would be surprised at how far a kind message will take you. Now, if there has been friction between the two of you, he may not be as receptive at first as you are hoping or expecting. Try to go into this idea without expectations. I know that is difficult. But depending on how deep the rut is, just keep in mind that you won't see a drastic change overnight. But if you keep at it, keep giving love and showing that you care, and that you appreciate him, eventually the ice will melt.

The same goes for men. If your woman is distant toward you, sending her a little sexy text or a reminder of your love for her will melt her heart. Although, again depending on the depth of the rut, I suggest sending the loving text first. Women are much softer than men, and just as it doesn't take much to excite a man sexually, it doesn't take much to cool a woman's anger for the man she loves. You just have to know the right words to say, and what buttons not to push. You cannot go wrong with telling your woman that she is beautiful, and that you love her.

Now, as I said before with men, she may not be receptive at first. But don't give up. If you are deep in a rut, or in the midst of an argument, your woman may be suspicious as to your intentions. In fact, her first thought may be that you have done something wrong, and it might actually worry her at first if her angry husband starts sending her loving texts out of the blue. However, don't be discouraged. Keep trying, and be persistent. One way to defuse the ticking bomb is to follow up with something like, "I have just been thinking about us and our relationship, and I want to try harder, because we matter to me. You matter to me." If you let your woman know how important she is to you and let her know that she and your relationship are your top priority, she will melt like butter. We women are relationship-oriented, and when you let us know that you are putting our relationship at the top of your priority list, you are now speaking our language.

The Quickie to the Rescue

While women draw the majority of their pleasure from slow, passionate sex, it's important not to underestimate the power of a quickie. The quickie, though not as pleasurable for a woman, is a great way to add spice to your sex life because the woman can gain her pleasure from the excitement and spontaneity of the moment. The quickie is physically pleasurably mostly for the man, because it allows him to completely enjoy himself without worrying about foreplay and the many steps it can take to please a woman. Sometimes a man can find himself a little strained in the sexual department because he has a lot to focus on: his endurance, whether or not he is hitting the spot, and whether or not his woman is enjoying herself enough to have an orgasm. But one of the aspects of sex that guys tend to worry about the most is their endurance. Sometimes they can focus so much on whether or not they are lasting long enough, that they end up losing their erection. The quickie allows your husband to forgo his inhibitions and just let free his animal urges.

A quickie can also be an excellent option for when the woman is not necessarily in the mood for sex or doesn't feel she has the energy to achieve an orgasm, but still wants to maintain that intimate connection and take care of her husband's needs. Women have trouble achieving orgasm more often than men do. A lot of the time, when we have had a stressful day at work, or we have issues with the kids weighing on our minds, our bodies tend to physically take on the stress and we end up wearing ourselves out. When this happens, it can sometimes be nearly impossible to achieve an orgasm, no matter how sexually aroused we are, which can lead to serious frustration, for the man as well as the woman.

A man will see his wife's frustration at her inability to achieve an orgasm, and his first thought is that it is his fault. One way to avoid this and still stroke his ego is to whisper to him that you just want to please him. You want to feel him inside of you, and you have to have him now. This makes him feel wanted, and lets him know that he doesn't have to bother with foreplay, while at the same time taking the pressure of achieving an orgasm or the temptation to fake one off of you. Plus, even if you find you are unable to achieve an orgasm this time around, there is just something about the rough passion your husband exhibits when he takes you in a quickie that is enough to leave you feeling a bit flushed.

While quickies are great for when you're not quite in the mood, they should really be saved for when you only have a few moments to spend with one another, you're out and about, or you just can't wait until you get home that evening. They shouldn't be your go-to option when the two of you are at home. If you always resort to having a quickie while the two of you are relaxing on the couch and watching television, then your sex life will quickly become routine and you will dig yourselves into a rut.

Quickies shouldn't be considered an option for getting sex out of the way so that you can enjoy your favorite show that is about to come on. Quickies should always be considered what they are: a quick and spontaneous option for sustaining your intimate connection throughout the day with your partner. And you should always strive to keep a quickie hot and passionate, never dull and lifeless.

As a woman, don't think that just because quickies are mainly designed for the man, that it means you can't gain pleasure from a quick tryst as well. Try carrying a small tube of minty lube in your purse, or keep it in your car when you know that you are going to be meeting up with your husband in the middle of the day. The minty lube gives off a sort of menthol feel to your genital area, giving you arousing sensations by itself, and helps to heighten your ability to have an orgasm. In addition, there are vibrators that you can buy that come in all sorts of discreet shapes and sizes. They even make vibrators that are disguised as lipstick cases. You can buy one of these discreet vibrators and bring it along with you for your next sexual tryst. Taking these few simple steps will help you to become aroused and even look forward to having a quickie with your husband.

There are several ways to make a romantic tryst ideal. First off, if you know your husband's lunch schedule, try sending him a quick, sexy text ahead of time, making him aware of your intentions. If you really want to get the ball rolling, try convincing him to meet up with you by first sneaking off into the bathroom at work and taking a little sexy preview for him. This will also help to serve as foreplay, when the day's schedule doesn't allow the time for any physical foreplay.

Make sure to dress the part. Part of what makes a quickie so endearing, is that it doesn't allow for each partner to get completely naked. The passion of having to have the other person right here, right now, leaves no time for completely undressing. In order to aid in the quickie process, try wearing skirts, preferably loose and flowy. Pencil skirts will work, just make sure to carry a little spray bottle of wrinkle releaser, otherwise you may find yourself searching for explanations to give your co-workers about the tussled look of your skirt. When you leave your clothing on, you heighten your husband's arousal by letting his imagination run wild. He will immediately be picturing you naked.

When you get in your car to meet with your husband, remove your panties before you drive to see him. This will heighten your sexual arousal. The feel of being without panties will excite you as you're driving, which will help to speed the whole process along. Even before you start driving, begin fantasizing about what lies ahead for you when you finally see your husband. Imagine meeting with him in secret, and having him take you in the bathroom at a restaurant, in a coat closet, or in the back seat of his car. By fantasizing ahead of time, you are actually giving yourself a little mental foreplay. As you are driving, you could even slide your hand to the now bare "v" between your legs. Feel your wetness and begin pleasing yourself on your way to see your husband. This will get the blood flowing to your vaginal area, and the more you stimulate your clit ahead of time, the easier it will be for you both to achieve orgasm. By taking these extra little steps to excite yourself, you will bring yourself halfway to orgasm by the time you see your husband. There is something insanely arousing about a man sliding his hands up your skirt and simply taking you, then and there, without the muss and fuss of foreplay. There is something primal about his quick, pounding thrusts that will renew the passion for both partners.

Amp Up the Daily Grind

The journey to revving up your sex life doesn't have to occur just in the bedroom. In actuality, it doesn't have to be just about sex, either. There are simple ways to subtly rekindle your partner's passion for you as you go throughout a normal day. As we go about our lives, we get used to the little quirks and habits that our partner possesses. We get so used to having our partner around and seeing him or her each day that we often let our guard down. And when we let our guard down, we let ourselves slip and often forget to put our best foot forward. When you see someone every day, and sleep next to him or her every night, it is near impossible to keep a little mystery in your relationships. Without mystery, the shiny newness tends to dull a lot more quickly. There are simple little steps we can take on a daily basis that will continue to keep the passion alive.

When you get up in the morning, before you even get out of bed, wake him up with a passionate kiss or a surprise blowjob. Leave it up to him whether or not he returns the favor, although most likely he will reciprocate with some oral sex or a little foreplay, and will probably even initiate sex. Plus, it will help to give him a little ego boost and surge of endorphins for the day.

When you get out of bed, make sure that you dress for work in front of him. When you're taking off your clothes, don't hide your body from your husband. He knows what you look like, so there's no need to shy away from being naked in front of him. Let him gaze upon your nakedness. This adds an extra little boost of sensuality to your morning, especially if he has just been awakened with a blowjob. Men are visual creatures and love to see the naked body of their woman, so let him gaze upon your body at his leisure. This can add extra spice to an otherwise ordinary morning.

When you do dress in front of him, catch his attention by choosing an out fit that shows off your figure. Don't pick something too tight, but something form-fitting that will help to enhance your curves, but still leaves a little to the imagination, and will have him wanting to see more of your naked body. If it happens to be a weekend, and the two of you are relaxing at home, change into a pair of yoga pants or tight bicycle shorts and a tight-fitting exercise shirt. If you have a workout routine, maybe do a few stretches in front of the television, and make sure that he has a front row seat of the view.

Try taking a little time to put on some make up and go the extra mile to look nice for your husband. Sometimes, especially with mothers who stay at home with young children, we tend to get a little busy and let the little things start slipping. When we are first married, everything about married life is still new and shiny. We want to please our spouse in the way we act, cook, dress, etc. But after a little while, we begin to get a little lazy. Maybe one day we don't do our hair, or we only put on make up every other day, then ever few days. But these little things, after a while, add up to a lot. A few days becomes once a week, then once a week becomes "on occasion." Putting on make up, fixing your hair, and dressing with care will not only turn his head, but it will give you a little boost in your confidence.

When you use the restroom, whether it's to shower, put on makeup, do your hair, or just plain conduct your business, leave the door closed. When we get used to living with another person, we just get lazy. It happens. Our secrets tend to go out the window, and that tends to happen in all areas of the marriage. Try and leave a little to the imagination. Don't use the restroom in front of your spouse, and make sure to keep the door closed. The only time you should make your partner privy to your bathroom activities is if you want to entice him into a little sexy shower time for two.

Remember to take a little time for yourself. Men love a woman with a little independence, and it can be hard to find ways to maintain your independence after marriage. When two people become one, they share everything together from the finances, to meals, to the bedroom. Make sure that every once in a while; you have your own thing going. Work on a crossword puzzle, or read a good book. If you are an artist, find time to paint or draw. Do a little writing. Find something that is your creative niche, and focus on it. When you have a little bit of talent that is separate from your husband and uniquely all your own, it helps you to maintain your individuality. Remember to never lose yourself in another person.

Find something that he may not have any interest in, but that interests you. Besides, when he sees you pursuing that talent instead of being completely focused on him, it will endear you to him that much more. Men desire to be the whole of a woman's pie, but they don't want to be. They enjoy the actual desire, the pursuit of a woman and the goal of being her everything, but they respect a woman who has her own thing going. When a man knows that he is not the whole pie of a woman's life, but a very big slice, it heightens his interest automatically increases his desire for her.

In the evening, take a little time out for a shower or to soak in the bathtub. Pour a little scented bubble bath or perfumed bath oils into the water, and soak for at least a half an hour, letting the oils absorb into your skin. If you're not in the habit of shaving your legs as often, try making shaving more of a priority. When you step out of the tub, add a little extra softness to your skin by rubbing on some scented lotion. When you put on the lotion, touching and caressing your own body will help to pump up your own arousal. Then, when you slip beneath the sheets, sleep naked. Let him feel your bare skin against his, and let his hand trail along the softness of your smooth legs. The feel of your skin beneath his touch combined with the luxurious scents of the bubble bath will heighten his arousal, and nine times out of ten, a woman who goes to bed naked is bound to get a little action from her man.

Passion is Everything

As I said before, nobody wants methodical. If you feel your heart isn't in your sex life, or your relationship as a whole, stop blaming your partner. The problem begins with you, and so does the solution. You chose your partner. They chose you. Don't look for comfort elsewhere. Make the choice to put your heart back into your relationship, and it will show in every area of your life.

You can have love without passion, but let's face it: it's boring. Passion is everything. It is the missing ingredient to spice up a tasteless dish. Without passion, what is worth it? Let the passion play begin.

Without passion, you and your partner find yourselves simply going through the motions. Sex becomes mechanical and lifeless. Passionless sex is dangerous sex, because when your heart is not into it, it allows your mind to wander off to places it shouldn't be. When you first get together with your spouse, the newness and the excitement combine to ignite a passionate fire. But over time, the fire tends to dim to a dull, glowing ember, and it is your job to stoke those embers and get that fire raging again. When you put the maintenance of passion high up on your priority list, you are ensuring the safety of your relationship.

One way to ignite passion in your woman is to tease her. A woman loves the feel of a light touch and your hands caressing her skin. Don't immediately jump to the goal line. Take your time, and with your fingertips, light a fever beneath her skin. The more gradual the buildup, the more sexual tension you create. And the more sexual tension that lies between the two of you, the more passionately those feelings will be expressed when you finally release that tension. Just as with everything, women take their time. A man is naturally direct and to the point, but a woman relishes in the excitement of the buildup. The more a woman becomes aroused, the more intense her passion for you becomes.

Think about why a man or a woman desires what they feel they cannot have, or how impatient they grow while waiting on something or someone that is taking their sweet time to arrive. It is because the longer you have to wait for something, the more your want and need for it increases. The more your desire for it increases, the sweeter it feels once your reward arrives. The same way, the more sexual tension you build between you and your partner, the more you drive each other wild with anticipation, the more passionately your desire for one another will play out, and the sweeter your release of that passion will be.

Depending on where you are at emotionally in your marriage, you may feel passion at varying levels. For instance, if you are in the midst of a fight or a long-standing argument, the passion you feel for your spouse may be repressed. Don't let anger stand in the way of physically expressing your love for your partner. Remember that anger itself is a form of passion and in fact, even if you and your partner find yourselves in a difficult down in your relationship, that anger can be redirected in order to help you to increase the strength of the bond with your partner.

Never use sex as a weapon. If you feel your relationship is in a rut, or you feel angry at your spouse, never withhold sex from them. It will only serve to erode the bond that you share. There is definite truth to the age-old advice to never go to sleep angry. It builds anger and resentment. It poisons your relationship, and withholding sex on top of it is relationship suicide. Over time, resentment builds. You may be angry at your partner for so many reasons, and maybe sex is the last thing you want to give them, but I have two words for you. Angry sex.

And I do not mean lying there like a cold brick while you let him have what he wants. No. I mean, if you are having trouble reigniting that passion you once shared because you have anger toward your spouse, then throw caution to the wind and give it all you have got in a good old-fashioned angry sex session. Ride him like a wild horse. There is no better cure for a long-standing argument than to fight it out naked. You could even take it back to the roleplaying idea, and spice it up. If you have a particularly difficult argument, one spouse can "punish" the other for either something they did, or just for the mere fact that they are being stubborn.

Part III:

LINES OF COMMUNICATION

Chapter Five:

Communicating Your Desires and Needs

Initiating Sex: Who's On First?

We discussed previously that men don't generally enjoy discussing their feelings. At the same time, they definitely do not enjoy talking about the existing problems in their relationships. Why? Because men are performance-oriented. When a woman brings up the problems that they have, even if she is just venting, a man's mind automatically comes to the conclusion that she is coming to him because she wants him to fix their problems, her problems, the world's problems. He is Mr. Fix-It, the world's handyman. When a woman comes to a man with either her problems or the problems that they are having, he automatically thinks that she is accusing him of doing wrong in some way. This is not always the case. If you are feeling stuck in a sexual right, and nothing changes, then nothing changes. So what do you do?

The best way to handle a delicate subject that has anything at all to do with a man's performance, especially sexual, is delicately. Send him direct signals, indirectly. Confusing? Let me explain. Without directly verbalizing your feelings regarding the sexual rut the two of you are in, ease into it. Begin by initiating sex with signals that are just direct enough for him to catch the hint. A good place to begin is focusing on what you wear...or don't...in front of your husband.

You can go out and buy a new negligée in his favorite color, or in a color that will incite his passion, such as red or a lacy black. You can also opt for sleeping in the nude. When you go to bed on a seemingly regular night, either slip on your brand new nighty, or ditch your comfy pajamas and slip beneath the sheets in the buff. Even if he isn't immediately in the mood, the feel of your bare skin next to his will entice him into sexual arousal, and will give him the chance to initiate sex.

If you choose to sleep naked, you may want to spray a few drops of perfume on beforehand. You could also take some time out of your evening to soak in a luxurious perfume bath, so that the aroma has time to seep into your skin. Then, once you slip beneath the covers, the scent, together with the sight and feel of your bare skin, will be completely intoxicating for him. You could also try slipping on one of his old t-shirts that he may have worn when you were dating, and wear it to bed without any underwear on. This will remind him of the days when the two of you couldn't keep your hands off of one another.

If you want to begin the seduction earlier in the evening, you can surprise him when he gets home from work by having his favorite meal cooked and ready on the table. It may sound cliché and too traditional, but men enjoy a good home cooked meal, especially one that was made with them in mind specifically. They don't say 'the way to a man's heart is through his stomach' for nothing! Make sure to add in a romantic wine to set the mood. If your husband isn't a wine guy, surprise him by having the fridge stocked with his favorite beer or beverage.

When your husband gets home, greet him with a few extra kisses, and one long, passionate kiss. This move is guaranteed to catch him off guard and right away he will begin tingling in his nether regions. Wrap your arms around his waist and snuggle into his neck, and make sure to show your excitement that he is finally home. When he sits down at the dinner table, make conversation, letting him know that you're genuinely interested to hear how his day went, and give him a little neck massage to ease the tension in his muscles. Just make sure to keep the questions to a minimum, so that he doesn't feel pressured to make conversation and end up wearing out. If he was previously too stressed or tired to think about sex, he will begin to relax. He will need time to let his mind and body naturally adjust to and get excited about the thought of a night of loving.

Make sure that when you are trying to convey the message that you want to have sex, that you aren't too assertive with your husband. If you find that you are initiating sex more than he is, it can create a problem because remember, men are hunters. They don't like to be the ones being pursued, this is a huge turn off for most men, and if they feel they are being pursued too aggressively or too much, they could lose interest in having sex. Remember to try to be evasive and keep a little bit of the mystery about you, rather than flat out asking if he would like to have sex. Dress up for him, wear a sexy outfit or sex lingerie in front of your husband, but make sure that he is pursuing you. In this way, you will peak his interest and gain his attention.

At the same time, if you find that he is initiating sex more often and you are finding yourself denying it more, this can also frustrate a man a great deal. In the same way that women value romance and want their husbands to make romance a more important aspect in their relationship, men get frustrated when their wives don't seem to feel that sex is as important in their relationship as it should be. The man needs to know that his woman desires him and wants him as much as he wants her. This will help him to maintain his desire to pursue her.

If your husband feels that you are rejecting him and neglecting his sexual needs too much, it can cause trouble in your marriage, and the sexual attraction you feel for one another will decline. If you lose your sexual attraction and erode that bond between the two of you, he may begin to look for other ways to satisfy his needs outside of the bedroom, and possibly outside of the marriage. To avoid these troubles, you want to make sure that you don't neglect your husband's needs, but that you maintain a balance by letting him initiate sex most of the time. When he gets to be the pursuer, his masculinity feels strengthened, which gives him an ego boost. When your husband feels more like a man, he regains his confidence and he becomes more willing and ready to have sex.

Sexual attraction can ebb and flow throughout the day, but if you maintain a little mystery and make sure that your husband knows that you desire him, it can help to reawaken his sexual arousal. It is much easier for a man to get his sexual desires up and running again than it is for a woman. This is mostly due to the fact that it doesn't take much to turn a man on. However, by making sex a high priority in your marriage, you can make it a goal to stay on track and actively work on maintaining that intimate connection. Sometimes making love cures a multitude of ills: exhaustion, emotional disconnection, and even lingering feelings of hurt from a recent or an unresolved argument.

Communicating Your Sexual Needs

Communication is the number one key to any lasting relationship. If your marriage is in a rut, communicating with your partner about your need and desire to have a little extra spice in your sex life can be difficult. More often than not, your partner's first thought will be that something they are doing or not doing is wrong. At the same time, communicating with your partner about your sexual needs is important because they cannot read your mind. It would be unfair to expect your partner to just know what you want in order to pull the two of you out of the sexual rut. It takes both parties equally working together to achieve the common goal of getting your relationship back on track. To avoid feelings of hurt and resentment, here are a few examples of communication guidelines for you and your partner to follow. Once you fix any existing problems of communication in your overall relationship, you can find that you will have a more open and free sexually fulfilling relationship as well.

Discussing problems is a necessary evil. Women are more open to communicating about the problems within the relationship than men are, but neither party is truly happy to discuss the issues between them. Remember that when you are having the discussion with your partner about the issues in your sexual relationship, try to not come across as if you are nagging your partner, and try to keep the blame out of what you have to say. Remember that your spouse is your life partner, and that you love them. Take care of their feelings by having them in mind when you say what you have to say. The tone of your voice as well as your body language can be a lethal combination, and if you're not careful, can send the wrong message of blame to your partner.

Be specific and direct with your words, when you are communicating your needs to your partner. Especially when you're speaking to your husband. Men don't like to beat around the bush; in fact, dragging out the conversation unnecessarily can be highly irritating for them. Be as direct as possible, and get to the point. If they feel you are trying to hint around, they will view it as your attempts to be coy, and therefore they will start to feel as if you're playing games with them. The best approach is to be straightforward and honest about what it is that you want from them.

Chapter Six:

ACTIONS SPEAK LOUDER THAN WORDS

Now that you have a plan, it's time to put it into action. This can be the most difficult part of getting your marriage out of the rut and back on track. Sometimes it can be difficult to communicate with our partner about our secret needs and desires. In the following chapter, we will discuss several tips for communicating your secret desires within the bedroom, so that your relationship will flourish outside of the bedroom.

Adjust Your Mindset

There is short distance between men and orgasms. Women, however, are a much more complicated story. One reason for this is the fact that men have a greater ability to compartmentalize their brains. They have this secret superpower called a one-track mind. Even when men are stressing over an event or situation in their life, they have an amazing ability to momentarily put it off in the dusty dark corners of their brain while they focus on long enough to put out the fires closest to their feet.

Women, however, are quite a bit different. Women worry about everything, everyone, and their neighbor's dog walker. More often than not, a woman will put everyone else above herself, and a woman possesses the natural ability to worry about a million tiny details at once, whether the subjects are related or not. Thus, it can be highly difficult for a woman to focus on the moment and stay one hundred percent sexually present.

Sex should not be treated like a burden for any partner, but it can be especially difficult for women to lose themselves in the moment and allow themselves to be completely consumed within the sexual experience when they have the stressors of daily life weighing heavily on their minds. The key to fixing this is for the woman to make the conscious decision to rearrange her priorities, and to view sex as a de-stressor.

As women, we have so much on our plate. We are natural nurturers, and therefore we tend to take on the role of taking care of the well-being of everyone in our path: our husbands, our children, our co-workers. The trouble is, we need to reorganize our mindset and put our emotional connection with our husbands first. We need to make that connection our number one priority because our children will one day grow up and move away, find loves and lives of their own, but our husbands are our life partners. We need to care for that relationship and maintain our connection with them, because without it, it would be difficult to face the struggles of every day life.

Sex with our husbands should be our go-to de-stressor. Our husbands should be the first thoughts in our minds when we think of ways to escape the drudgery of everyday life. When we have sex with our husbands, we need to leave work at work, and the problems that we face on a daily basis outside of the bedroom. Realize that your to-do list will get done in time, but the most important thing that should fill up the spaces in your mind is maintaining the connection you share with your husband. Change your mindset. Become enthusiastic about sex and intimacy with your man. With the right attitude, you can increase the passion you feel for your spouse by increasing your enthusiasm toward sex.

Body Image

You have to not only train your mind to have the right attitude toward sex, but you must train your train your mind to view yourself in a positive light, as well. Sometimes when we look at ourselves in the mirror, we tend to pick ourselves apart, and we enhance our insecurities. We analyze our stretch marks; we stare at our stomachs and our thighs until we're sure that extra pound or two that we think we've gained is visible to everyone who crosses our path. Our body image can play a huge part in why we have less sex with our partners. But when a man looks at the woman he loves, he does not see the flaws she sees. The majority of the time, when a man develops a wandering eye, it isn't because we have gained a few of those pesky extra pounds. It is because we become so self-conscious that we tend to let that stand in our way of giving him sexual attention and he feels neglected. Remember that men love a woman with confidence, and even if you don't quite feel it one hundred percent of the way, if you let your confidence shine through, I promise you that is what he will see.

Stop allowing your own insecurities to hinder your relationship. If you struggle with your self-confidence, there are still several sex positions that you can try that will help those (often imaginary) problem areas that you are so worried about. Reverse cowgirl is a great position to try if you're worried about extra pounds around your tummy and thighs. If these areas are weighing on your mind, facing away from him will help you to ease up and relax a little, so that you can let down your inhibitions. Doggy style works great for hiding these problem areas as well. In addition, if you happen to feel like you have what my mother calls "bingo arms" with a little extra jiggle, having sex in the doggy style position helps to hide your arms as well.

If you happen to be a little more self-conscious about your backside, a great position that will hide your behind is a variation of the cowgirl position, Have your husband sit up on the bed, or in a chair, and climb on top of him into his lap. This position gives him a great view of your breasts, which he can caress while allowing for deep penetration while you rock back and forth on him. Spooning is another good position for hiding your tummy, while still maintaining the feeling of being intimate.

Enjoying a little oral foreplay, particularly in the sixty-nine position, is a great way to hide your problem areas as well, as neither of you can really see or will be paying much attention to the rest of your bodies. When you are lying on your back while he is performing oral sex on you, your arms will be hidden, and lying on your back helps to keep everything "staying put." And most of all, he will have a great view of your body that he will love.

Kegel Exercises

For women, there is a simple exercise that you can practice at home that will not only improve your exercise, but will help to improve your overall well-being. By practicing these exercises, you can increase the blood flow to your genital area, and help to strengthen the intensity of both sexual arousal and your orgasm.

Kegel exercises strengthen your pubic muscles and when a woman clenches those muscles during sex, she can increase the intensity of her orgasm. Any exercise that focuses on these muscles will help to improve your sex life, but as an example, a great exercise to get you started is to lie flat on your back, with your legs about shoulder width-apart and you knees bent.

Think about the feeling of your muscles contracting as you orgasm. While maintaining your breathing throughout this exercise, focus on manually contracting and releasing your pelvic muscles in rapid succession, simulating the aftermath of an orgasm. As you work to contract your muscles, gradually build up the length of time you hold the contraction and as well as for how long you release the tension. The beauty of this exercise is that it can be practiced anywhere: at your desk during working ours or while you're at home, relaxing on the couch. These exercises will help to build your control over your muscular contractions and as you master this exercise on your own, it will help to increase your concentration on your pelvic muscles during sex.

Sexual Foods

There are certain foods that, believe it or not, can help put you in the mood for sex. The most common food that helps to boost your sex life is one that the majority of the population is already aware of: raw oysters. Raw oysters not only act as a natural aphrodisiac, but they also increase the quality of a man's sperm. Another food that affects a man's sperm is pineapple. If a man eats pineapple before getting down and dirty, it helps to make his sperm taste better for when you incorporate oral sex into your foreplay.

Avocados are another food that helps to enhance your sex life. Avocadoes are good for your heart, and they help to get the blood pumping throughout your body. They increase libido and help to give you more energy. Eggs are a low calorie option for helping to boost your sex drive, as they are high in protein. They are also packed with amino acids, and another heart healthy food source. Any foods that are healthy and good for your heart are going to help boost your sex drive, because they help to battle against erectile dysfunction in men.

Once you educate yourself on the list of foods that can help you in your journey to improving your sex life, you can get creative and have a little fun. Surprise your man with a romantic dinner, complete with a buffet of foods chockfull of vitamins that help to increase your sex drive. Try adding a side salad packed with nuts, such as cashews and almonds, which are high in zinc, and fruit such as watermelon, which acts as a natural male enhancement and can have the same effects on the male body as Viagra. For desert, try topping off the dinner with some chocolate covered strawberries to ignite the passion. You can settle down with your spouse for an evening at home, pop in a romantic movie, and let the romance begin.

Setting the Mood

Sometimes, a good old-fashioned candlelit dinner is enough to set the scene for romance. All it really takes to turn an evening for two at home from lukewarm to rock-your-socks off spectacular is a little effort. Here are a few simple steps that require minimal effort while maximizing your chances of reigniting the passion in your sex life.

Lighting is important when setting the stage for romance. When you dim the lights and light a few candles, the flame of the candles creates a soft orange glow, and the resulting romantic ambiance is perfect for enhancing the feel of intimacy. An extra step to take is to make sure that you light a few scented candles with soft, heady, sensual aromas. The setting provides inspiration for regaining your intimate connection.

It is always good to have a list of mood music on hand. The perfect music will add sensuality to the ambiance of the setting. Depending on what type of sex you plan on having, your choice of music selection should match your mood. If you plan on making love, and making the evening all about the romance, your choice of music should reflect soft, sexy rhythms, for example. You can move the tryst into the bedroom, or you can mix things up by changing the location. It might be a nice, romantic surprise to take a sensual bubble bath with your lover. Soaking in the tub together and taking turns washing each other is not only erotic, but it is also incredibly intimate, as it demonstrates each partner taking care of each other.

Make sure that you and your partner leave your phones out of the bedroom. Disconnect from the outside world for the night, and direct your attention solely on your spouse. Setting the right mood before the action takes place will help to clear your mind of the day's stressors and help you to focus completely on the sensual night ahead.

Foreplay

So much thought and attention should go into foreplay, and unfortunately, it does not always get the consideration that it deserves. Because men are goal-oriented, most tend to focus on the end result while paying little to know attention to the preshow. Foreplay is not simply about oral sex alone. There are so many important elements to the makeup of foreplay. Foreplay is the most essential element to spice up your sex life. Foreplay, when done right, helps to ignite passion and set the mood. It goes a long way in helping to prepare your spouse for intercourse, and without incorporating foreplay into your sexy time, the sex itself can be painful for one or both parties.

As I have stated before, men tend to want to get right to the point. However, foreplay should be done slowly in order to increase the sexual tension, and to absorb everything part of the moment. Here are a few simple tips to spicing up the preshow, so that you and your partner can experience an explosive finale:

You've already set the mood. The candles are lit. The scent of sex fills the air as soft music plays in the background. You've just finished dinner. It is time. Stand up and walk over to your spouse, your lover. Take their hand and lead them to the location of your choosing: perhaps the bathroom for a sensuous bubble bath. Or, since the kids are asleep, maybe you have to have them, right there on the dining room table. Slowly grab your partner to you, and pull them in for an intimate kiss. Remind them of how it felt when you were first so into each other, you couldn't manage to keep your hands to yourself.

Start slowly undressing one another, picking up the pace as the passion builds. To increase the tension, you can caress your partner through their clothes. The material of their clothes will help to create friction and build tension. You should increase the speed with which you undress each other as you go, but make sure not to rush too much. Remember that the final climax will be that much sweeter the longer you have to wait for it. Rushing through foreplay without giving your libido the chance to really get fired up can lead to disappointment. It takes a moment to truly take in the atmosphere around you, and staying determined to take things slow will also help you to build patience.

As you undress your wife, you can heighten her sensitivity by placing tiny kisses in some of her erogenous zones. Place a kiss at the little dip in the base of her neck, pull her hair aside and kiss the side of her neck, and leave a trail traveling up her neck and along her jawline. The more soft kisses you leave, the more she will "heat up". Remember, women loved to be teased, so the more sweet torture you force her to endure, the more you will drive her crazy with passion for you.

Although quickies are another thrilling way to spice up your sex life in the middle of a rough day when you and your partner are pressed for time, remember that that having a quickie is not your goal here. You want to draw out your partner's passion from deep within them. If you want to get rough and wild later on, rough sex is always exciting, but you must build up to it. Continue leaving kisses along your spouse's jawline and tease your way to her lips. The more you can manage to tease her, the better. Once your lips finally meet, you will be surprised at the strength of the passion behind her kiss.

Use your tongue to softly part her lips, and take her bottom lip between yours, and maybe even lightly, again I say, lightly, nibble at her lip. Slipping your wife the tongue is romantic, but you don't want to choke her with it, and you don't want to bite her so hard that you hurt her. Nothing kills the mood quite like intending to be kinky, but drawing blood instead. However a little nibble here and there is a good technique to add heat to the moment. There is something about a love bite that exhibits an almost animal need for your mate, and when it comes to sex, there's nothing hotter than forgoing the appearance of being civilized and getting back to our basic, primal urges.

Remember to not only let your partner know your need for them through your actions, but through the sounds you make as well. Making sure to moan and let your partner hear as well as feel your arousal helps to heighten theirs. Once you've undressed your partner, you can continue to place kisses all along their body and when you do, make sure to moan against their skin. This creates tiny little vibrations, causing goose bumps to form and heightening their arousal. Once you and your partner are fully nude, you can work your way, with your lips, to their genital area, and get down to business with everyone's favorite part of foreplay: sexual stimulation, both manually and orally.

A few simple tips to remember when you and your partner are engaging in foreplay: don't neglect the often-overlooked pleasure spots. First and foremost, your scalp. When you are going in for that passionate kiss with your spouse, remember to run your fingers through their hair. With your fingertips, lightly massage their scalp. The scalp too is made up of tons of tiny little nerve endings, and it can feel quite pleasurable when your scalp is caressed. Plus, men love to play with your hair. They seem to be fascinated by the feel and scent of a woman's hair.

Remember what we discussed earlier? Never underestimate the sensitive spot at the back of her neck. Softly kissing this area is guaranteed to drive your woman insane with pleasure. Don't neglect her ears. Kiss your way from the base of her neck to the backs of her ears, making sure to nibble and lightly suck on her earlobes. As your kissing and nibbling, try lightly blowing against her neck and the backs of her ears. The cool air on the slight wetness of your kisses is going to give her goose bumps, and heighten her arousal.

If you really want to kick off the foreplay, a good way to initiate sex is giving your woman a back rub. The back is highly sensitive, and caressing a woman's back helps to tease her and is a sure fire way of turning her on. Softly stroke, kiss, nibble, and massage your way from her neck down to her ankles, paying particular attention to her behind, and making sure to reach through and stroke her clit. Back rubs are a great way to jump start sex, especially if it has been a while since you and your spouse have been intimate. If your spouse has had a long, rough day at work, they are most likely not going to turn down a back rub and more often than not, back rubs don't end up as innocently as they begin.

Don't underestimate the power of your legs. Even if you don't feel you have great legs, there is just something about a pair of legs that men again find fascinating; they can't keep their hands off of them. The backs of the knees are an especially sensitive area, and when caressed, the teasing sensation will heighten a woman's arousal and drive her a little wild. Her toes and ankles are sensitive erogenous zones as well; so don't forget to caress them softly. You can also kiss and nibble at the Achilles part of her heel. Begin in this spot, and plant kisses all along the lengths of her legs, paying particular interest to the backs of her knees. Then carefully kiss your way to her panties, working your way back down her legs as you take them off. This is another sensitive area that is sure to drive her crazy

Another area you should make sure to pay a little attention to is her tummy. You can take your fingertip and lightly circle her belly button, caressing it softly and even dipping your finger inside. The nerves in your belly button run like a direct line to your genital area, so the belly button is highly sensitive, and teasing this area instantly heightens a woman's sexual arousal. You can even circle your spouse's belly button with your tongue softly, gently inserting your tongue. This is highly enticing, as it will remind her instantly of oral sex.

Let's switch over to a man's sensitive areas for a moment. Ladies, if you really want to fire up your man for a little sexy time, lightly begin stroking his bare chest. Tease your way down his stomach, again paying particular attention to his belly button, as men are just as sensitive in this region as we are. Play with his belly button for a few moments before trailing your way with your fingertips down to the waistband of his pants. Here, you can have a little teasing fun. Take a little time exploring the "V" shape at the top of his pants. Begin lightly stroking the area with your fingertips, and then begin adding a little pressure, rubbing the area lightly. Next to directly grabbing a hold of your man's nether regions, teasing this area fires him up just as quickly. It also helps to teach him a little patience. Touching this area will fire him up fast, so make sure to tease him as much as possible, going slowly, until he grabs you and turns you over, ready for action.

A little known body part that women often forget to pay attention to are men's hands. Men love to have their hands rubbed softly. Try kissing his palm as you caress his hands with your fingertips, working your way to his fingers with your lips. Take each finger in your mouth, and slowly begin sucking on each one, beginning at the tip and working your way down to its hilt, just like with his penis. This turns a man on because it puts your oral skills on display for him, and he will watch in fascination, as it reminds him of when you give him a blowjob. Just be prepared for him to grab your head and force it down to his groin.

AFTERWORD

This book is meant to be a guide for providing fun, easy, and helpful tips to rekindling that flame, whether it is old, worn out, dying down, or just getting blown around in the wind and trying to hang on. This book is geared toward both men and women, and its chapters are meant to be short so that the task of reconnecting with your spouse doesn't come off as a daunting one. Reconnecting with your partner and making the fire burn once again; even stronger this time around should be a fun and exciting journey that the two of you impart on together...naked.

As I have said several times in this book, the woman is more likely to become aware of problems in the relationship, especially in the sexual department, therefore this book is mainly written with women in mind. If you are a woman and you are holding this book in your hands, then that means that there are one or more problems that you are desperately seeking a solution for. Remember that, should you decide to share this book with your partner, you should find a way to do so gently. Problems anywhere in a relationship can be difficult to address, but specifically problems in the bedroom, if not handled delicately, can come off as a blow to your husband's ego.

Instead, you should think about approaching the subject from an excited standpoint. Maybe you can try telling him that you want to explore fun and sexy things that the two of you can try together, and if he gets the impression you are just wanting to try something new instead of trying to talk about your problems, then he will be more likely to take a look at this book. At the end of the day, the only tools you really need in order to get the fires of passion burning again are the imagination and determination of both partners.

When it comes down to it, saving your relationship is a decision. Rekindling the romance between the two of you is a matter of choice. You made the decision to share your life with your spouse. You chose them, and they chose you. The problem is, choosing your spouse is not a once in a lifetime event. Choosing your spouse is a choice you must wake up everyday and make all over again, and you mustn't assume that because you are still resting your head on the pillow next to theirs, that they are constantly aware of your affection for them. Don't assume that he or she knows that you love them. Women especially want to be reminded that we are yours; not because we have to be legally, but because you want us. Take time to remind your partner how much they mean to you, and every day, choose your partner all over again.

Forget the stressors of every day life and remember that one day, when you look back, it won't matter whether or not you made it to work on time that day. It won't matter what color of shirt you wore, if your husband accidentally spilled coffee on your new skirt that morning, or if you weren't able to catch your favorite television show that evening. In fact, I guarantee you; you most likely won't even recall the name of your favorite television show when your time on earth is coming to an end. But I can promise you, that you will remember one name in those last days, and that will be the name of the one you either chose to fight to keep with all of your heart and soul, or the one you let walk away because you couldn't handle putting in a little effort. Falling in love is beyond our control, but staying in love with the same person requires work that can only be done by first making the choice to re-commit to your marriage. Make that choice, and let your partner know that you choose them now, and all the days to come. Now go out there, and have yourself a passionate love affair…with your spouse!

Don't Stop Here, Keep going…Bonus Ahead.

BONUS FOR THE LADIES

A must watch - The Single Most Important Thing To A Man . . .

It takes a lot to shock me, but this video made me go "Wow."

===>> **http://tinyurl.com/l8usq4y**

It's by this guy named James Bauer and it explains the single most important thing to a man when it comes to having a relationship.

===>> **http://tinyurl.com/l8usq4y**

If you think guys are "complicated" or "hard to figure out" you really need to watch this video now.

Your Fire Lover,

Rochelle Foxx

P.S. After he reveals the "most important thing," James shows you how to trigger this one critical emotion in your guy to draw him closer to you and make him almost addicted to you long term.

What I really love about what James says is that it's not manipulative or "game playing."

===>> **http://tinyurl.com/l8usq4y**

BONUS FOR THE GUYS

(Ladies you will LOVE this too)

Below is my #1 Recommended Program for my ALL Male Clients.

I have never recommended any other program over this one. Listen to me guys…

3 Things You Can Do To A Woman To Give Her The Best Orgasms Of Her Life

Do your wife a favor and go to this link.
http://tinyurl.com/k6k6xjf

Conclusion

Thank you again for downloading this book!

If you enjoyed this book, then I'd like to ask you for a favor, would you be kind enough to leave a review for this book on Amazon? It'd be greatly appreciated!

Help us better serve you by sending questions or comments to rochellefoxxbooks@gmail.com - Thank you!

Made in the USA
San Bernardino, CA
14 December 2017